52 Weeks of
Family Night

52 Weeks of Family Night

Fast and Easy Lessons for
Young Families

Tamara Baggett

DESERET
BOOK

SALT LAKE CITY, UTAH

Illustrations by Julie Young

Text © 2005 Tamara Baggett
Art © 2005 Deseret Book Company

Library of Congress Cataloging-in-Publication Data

Baggett, Tamara.
    52 weeks of family night : fast and easy lessons for young families / Tamara Baggett.
        p. cm.
    ISBN 1-59038-401-6 (pbk.)
    1. Mormon families. 2. Family—Religious life. 3. Christian education—Home training. 4. Church of Jesus Christ of Latter-day Saints—Doctrines—Study and teaching. 5. Mormon Church—Doctrines—Study and teaching. I. Title: Fifty two weeks of family night. II. Title.
    BX8643.F3B34 2005
    249—dc22
                                                                      2004021690

Printed in the United States of America   18961
R. R. Donnelley, Crawfordsville, IN

10   9   8   7   6   5

Contents

How to Use This Book

This book was written to help families with younger children realize the rich blessings promised to those who hold regular family home evening. Here are some suggestions on using this book:

• You will find fifty-two squares in the back of the book. Each square has a number and a small picture. Photocopy the pages and cut the squares out. (Note: You may want to color the pictures and laminate the pages with the squares before you begin cutting.) Once the squares are cut, put them into a bag and store them with the book.

• When it's time for family home evening, have someone randomly choose a square out of the bag, and have a child hold the square so everyone can see it. Look at the number and picture on the square, and then turn to the chapter that coincides with that number. You'll see that the chapter includes a scripture to review, a recommended song to sing, and a short lesson to read aloud to the family. (When a song reference includes the initials CS, it indicates the *Children's Songbook* published by the Church in 1989. If a song has several verses, you may choose to sing just one or two.)

• Have someone conduct by assigning other family members to lead the song, find the scripture, and read the lesson. (A typical family home evening could include the following: opening song, opening prayer, lesson, closing song, closing prayer, refreshments, and activity. You may want to put these elements of home evening on a chart and rotate the opportunity to do each.)

• Family home evening will be most effective if you talk about what you're reading. You may want to ask questions during the reading or at the end.

• If you have older children with longer attention spans, every child may wish to participate and choose more than one lesson to discuss that evening.

Regular family home evening can be one of the greatest gifts parents can give to their children. The First Presidency has said: "We promise you great blessings if you will follow the Lord's counsel and hold regular family home evenings. We pray constantly that parents in the Church will accept their responsibility to teach and exemplify gospel principles to their children. May God bless you to be diligent in this most important responsibility" ("Message from the First Presidency," *Family Home Evening Resource Book* [1983], iv).

These lessons will help you make family home evening work for your family. With the help of this book, you can make sure home evening is a learning experience for even very young children. In addition, these family home evening lessons can also be a wonderful asset to sacrament meeting or Primary talks.

•1•
Prayer

Doctrine and Covenants 68:28
"I Pray in Faith" (CS, 14)

Elder Russell M. Nelson, one of the Twelve Apostles, said, "Father in Heaven wants to hear from His children. Through prayer, we can show our love for God. And He has made it so easy. We may pray to him any time. No special equipment is needed. We don't even need to charge batteries or pay a monthly service fee.

"Some people pray only when confronted with personal problems. Others don't pray at all. . . . Prophets have long told us to pray humbly and frequently."*

Why do we pray? We pray to talk to our Heavenly Father. When you want to tell your mom or dad something, you get close to them and talk to them. Our Heavenly Father wants to hear from us every day. When Jesus was here on this earth he taught us to pray.

When should we pray? We should pray every day in the morning and again at night. We should pray when we are about to eat, and any time we feel thankful, happy, sad, or afraid. We also can pray when we need help or for others when they need help. We can always keep a prayer in our hearts.

How do we pray? The most respectful way to pray is on our knees, with our arms folded. When we are at church we do not need to kneel. If we are away from home and we need to talk to our Heavenly Father, we can say a prayer in our minds and he will hear us.

When we say a prayer, we should first address our Heavenly Father. Second, we need to thank our Heavenly Father for everything he has given us. Third, we can ask our Heavenly Father for anything we may need from him. Last, we close in the name of Jesus Christ.

---

*"Sweet Power of Prayer," *Ensign,* May 2003, 7.

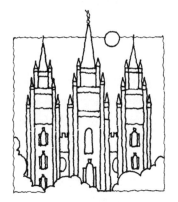

•2•
Temples

Psalm 27:4

"I Love to See the Temple" (CS, 95)

Temples are places of love and beauty. Heavenly Father has always commanded his people to build temples.

A temple is a special place where we can learn more about our Heavenly Father and Jesus. In the temple, we are taught Heavenly Father's plan for us. We are able to perform sacred ordinances, such as baptisms for the dead and marriages for eternity.

Heavenly Father wants all of his children to have the opportunity to go to his temples. There we can receive blessings that will help us become more like our Heavenly Father and help us return to live with him someday. There we can be sealed together as eternal families. We can also perform the ordinances necessary to provide our ancestors with these same blessings. When we go to the temple and do temple work, we are helping people in the spirit world to be able to live with Heavenly Father.

President Gordon B. Hinckley has given us this testimony of the temple: "Reason demands that the family relationship shall continue after death. The human heart longs for it. The God of heaven has revealed a way whereby it may be secured. The sacred ordinances of the house of the Lord provide for it."*

---

*"Why These Temples?" *Ensign,* August 1974, 40.

•3•
Baptism

3 Nephi 11:33
"When I Am Baptized" (CS, 103)

In The Church of Jesus Christ of Latter-day Saints, we are baptized when we reach the age of eight. Our prophets teach us that the age eight is important because this is when we become accountable and responsible for our actions. People can also be baptized when they are older than eight if they learn of the Church and want to join it at an older age.

Baptism is important because our Heavenly Father commands it. When we are baptized we receive many blessings from our Heavenly Father. Through repentance and baptism, we can be cleansed of our sins. The ordinance of baptism can be performed in many different types of places. But wherever it takes place, the one being baptized must be immersed in water, and the baptism must be performed by someone who has priesthood authority from God.

Baptism is the beginning of a new life for each of us. It can be a wonderful life of purpose. When we are baptized, we covenant with the Lord to serve him and keep his commandments. We covenant to remember Jesus and to be a part of his family. When we do that, he promises to send the Holy Ghost to help us.

A covenant is a promise we make with our Heavenly Father. When we make covenants, we show our love for God and promise to obey him.

Each time you take the sacrament, you will be reminded of the covenant or promise you made when you were baptized. As you follow Jesus' teachings, you will be keeping your promise.

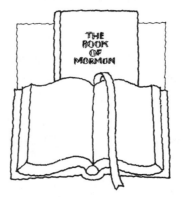

•4•
Joseph Smith

Joseph Smith–History 1:14–17, 33–34
"On a Golden Springtime" (CS, 88)

When Joseph Smith was fourteen years old, he did not know which church to join, so he went to the woods to pray for help in his decision. As he was praying he saw a very bright light. In the light were Heavenly Father and Jesus Christ. Heavenly Father pointed to Jesus and said, "This is my Beloved Son. Hear Him!" Joseph Smith asked which church he should join. The Son, Jesus Christ, told him not to join any of them.

Three years went by. Then one night as Joseph prayed in his bedroom, he saw another bright light, and in the light he saw an angel. The angel told Joseph that his name was Moroni and that God had a great work for him to do. He told Joseph Smith about a book written by a people who lived in America many years ago. Joseph learned that the book was about the gospel of Jesus Christ, and that it would help him to learn more about Jesus and his work on the earth.

Moroni told Joseph Smith that the book was hidden in a hill not very far from him, under a big rock. The name of the hill was Cumorah. Joseph went to the hill Cumorah and found the place Moroni had described. Joseph moved the big rock and found a stone box. Inside the box was a book, but it did not look like the books we have now. The pages were made of gold, and they had engraved writing on them. The writing was in a language Joseph Smith did not know.

Moroni would not let Joseph take the gold plates but told him to come back each year. After four years Joseph was able to take the plates. God helped Joseph Smith translate the plates, while a friend wrote the words down. The book that Joseph Smith translated is what we now call the Book of Mormon.

•5•
Keeping Promises

Alma 24:15-19

"I Want to Live the Gospel" (CS, 148)

When King Mosiah's sons went out as missionaries, many Lamanites joined the Church. After they discovered the gospel, they didn't want to fight anymore. So they set aside their swords, spears, and other weapons. These righteous Lamanites called themselves the people of Ammon. Ammon was one of the sons of Mosiah.

Many Lamanites hated the people of Ammon and wouldn't believe in Jesus Christ, so the Lamanites decided to fight them. When Lamoni's father, the king of the righteous Lamanites, learned what the wicked

Lamanites were planning to do, he reminded his people that they had once been wicked and had killed many people. But when they joined the Church, they repented and were forgiven. The king was afraid that if they killed again, they might not be forgiven.

Since they wanted to keep God's commandments and remain clean, they threw their swords and other weapons in a hole and covered them up. They then made a covenant with God that they would never fight or kill anyone again, even if they lost their own lives.

Soon the wicked Lamanites attacked, but the people of Ammon would not fight. Instead they knelt down to pray. The Lamanites killed many people of Ammon, but when the Lamanites saw that the people of Ammon would not fight, many of them stopped fighting and threw their own weapons down. They repented and joined the righteous people of Ammon.

Even when their lives were threatened, the people of Ammon kept their promise not to fight. Because they were righteous and kept their promise, Heavenly Father blessed those who died that they would have great happiness in the spirit world, where they would live until their spirit and body were reunited in the resurrection. And he blessed many others to know that the Church was true.

•6•
Jesus Christ Heals a Blind Man

John 9:1–7

"My Heavenly Father Loves Me" (CS, 228)

Miracles were a part of Jesus Christ's life when he was on the earth. One Sabbath day he and his disciples came upon a man who had been blind since he was born. Jesus Christ loved the people, and he wanted to help this man. He spat on the ground and made mud. Then he took this mud and put it on the man's eyes. He told the man to go and wash his eyes in the pool of Siloam. The man obeyed Christ. After he finished washing his eyes he was able to see. It was a great miracle.

When the people heard that he could see, they wanted to know how it happened. After the man told the others what had happened, the people took him to the Pharisees, and they questioned him. The man again told the story. The Pharisees became angry and began to argue with each other. The law in the land was that it was a sin for anyone to work on the Sabbath day. Some of the Pharisees said that healing on the Sabbath was work, and that Jesus must be a sinner. Others said, If a person is a sinner, he would not be able to heal.

The Pharisees decided that maybe the man had never really been blind. They decided to talk to his parents. His parents told them that he really had been born blind and that now he could see.

The Pharisees then told the man that he should thank God for healing him but to believe that Jesus Christ was a sinner. The man said, "If this man [Jesus] were not of God, he could do nothing" (John 9:27, 31, 33). The Pharisees became angrier and threw the man out of their presence.

When Jesus heard what the Pharisees had done to the young man, he asked him if he believed in the Son of God. He told Christ that he believed, and he worshipped him.

Miracles from Christ are part of the blessings we receive from God if we believe in him.

•7•
Pioneers

Doctrine and Covenants 136:5–7
"Whenever I Think about Pioneers" (CS, 222)

After the Prophet Joseph Smith was killed by wicked men, the members of the Church knew that they were in danger. Brigham Young, their new leader, led the members from Nauvoo, Illinois, to Winter Quarters, Nebraska, and from there to the Salt Lake Valley in Utah. The entire journey was more than a thousand miles long. Between 1847 and 1869 about seventy thousand members of the Church made the trek across mountains, rivers, and treacherous terrain to seek religious freedom. We call these wonderful and faithful people *pioneers*.

The pioneers traveled in groups and used covered wagons and handcarts as they crossed the plains. Most of the pioneers walked the entire way. The covered wagons were used for the elderly, the sick, and very young children. It was a difficult journey, and many did not make it to the Salt Lake Valley.

The journey of some of the pioneers started far across the ocean in other countries, before they even reached America. They were all in search of the same thing—to be able to worship the true God in peace and to gather with other Saints.

The first company of Mormon pioneers, led by Brigham Young, entered the Great Salt Lake Valley on July 24, 1847. Brigham Young looked at the beautiful valley and announced, "This is the right place." It had been a long trip, but at last there was a place where The Church of Jesus Christ of Latter-day Saints could grow in peace.

The pioneers left a legacy of faith, love for one another, and love for God. We now celebrate Pioneer Day each year on July 24 to remember and honor the faith and sacrifice of these courageous pioneers.

•8•
Jonah and the Great Fish

Jonah 1:17–2:4
"Repentance" (CS, 98)

A long time ago there lived a man named Jonah, and he was a prophet of God. The Lord asked Jonah to go to a city called Nineveh, to preach to the people and tell them to repent. Jonah was afraid that the people would laugh at him, so he got on a boat going to Tarshish instead.

As the boat was sailing, a great storm arose. It was tossing the boat around so much that the men aboard thought it would break into pieces. The other men on the boat asked Jonah why this terrible storm had come upon them. Jonah told them it was because he had made God angry by disobeying him. Jonah said that they should cast him into the sea because it was his fault. The men tried to row to safety, but they were unable to. Finally they cast Jonah into the sea. Jonah probably thought he would drown, but the Lord had prepared a great fish to swallow Jonah.

While he was in the belly of the fish, Jonah prayed to the Lord and was sorry that he had disobeyed. He repented and agreed to go to Nineveh and preach to the people. After three days, the fish spit Jonah out onto dry land. Jonah then went to Nineveh and preached to the people. They also repented, and the Lord was pleased.

•9•
Jesus and the Atonement

Luke 22:41–44
"He Sent His Son" (CS, 34)

In the last days of his life, Jesus Christ gathered with his disciples for what is called "the last supper." There he taught them about the sacrament, telling them that the sacrament would be a reminder that he would suffer, bleed, and die for the sins of the world.

After the last supper, Jesus and his disciples walked to the Garden of Gethsemane. He went a short distance from his disciples and began to pray. He knew that the time had come to pay the price for our sins. He asked Heavenly Father to bless him, because he could feel the weight of the sins of all the people who would ever live on the earth. It was such a great burden that he bled from every pore.

Early the next morning, Jesus was arrested for claiming to be the Son of God. He was beaten with whips and made fun of. A crown of thorns was pushed on his head. He was then nailed to a cross, where he suffered for six hours. Then Jesus died. After Jesus died on the cross, his body was taken by one of his followers and put in a tomb. On the third day, he rose from the dead, a resurrected being.

No one can fully understand what pain our Savior endured. Because he took upon himself all the sins and pains of the world, he knows and understands our trials. His atonement was an act of love for which we should be more grateful than for any other blessing or gift of God. Jesus gave his life to pay for our sins so that if we repent, we can be forgiven and be clean again. And because Jesus had power to be resurrected, he will help us to be resurrected too.

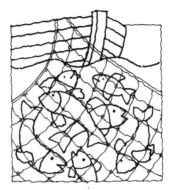

•10•
Fishers of Men

Matthew 4:18-20

"Lord, I Would Follow Thee" (Hymns, 220)

In the time of Jesus, fishing was very important. The people who lived near the Sea of Galilee used fishing as a means to make a living. And of course fish was one of the main things the people there ate.

Jesus was familiar with fishing and knew many fishermen. He called some of them to become his followers. He said he wanted them to become fishers of men. To become a fisher of men is to follow Jesus and to tell others about his gospel.

Most people fish with a pole. But people who fish for a living often use a net. That's what fishermen in the time of Jesus used. The fishermen would row or sail out into a lake or sea, drop large nets into the water, and then take the boat back toward the shore. As they went, the nets would gather fish.

Both then and now, a good fisherman doesn't give up easily. If the fish are not biting, he may try a different place or try different bait. A good fisherman will keep at it until he catches a fish.

We must be good gospel fishermen if we want to please the Lord. We must follow Christ and tell others about his gospel. Missionaries are some of the great fishermen in the Church today. We should all be missionaries.

"Follow me," Jesus said, "and I will make you fishers of men." We need to put forth time, effort, and diligence to become "fishers of men" and teach the gospel of Jesus Christ.

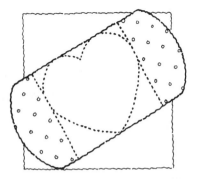

•11•
The Good Samaritan

Luke 10:30-37
"I'll Walk with You" (CS, 140)

At the time of Jesus, many Jewish people felt that they were better than other groups of people. For example, Jewish children were taught not to like the Samaritan children, and Samaritan children were taught not to like Jewish children. Jesus wanted all people to love one another, so he taught this parable.

One day a Jewish man was traveling from Jerusalem to Jericho. Some thieves attacked him and took all his money and clothes. They beat him up and left him on the road to die.

Then a Jewish priest came down the road. He was

a leader in his church, and he should have stopped and helped the man. Instead, he crossed the street to the other side of the road and walked on by.

A little while later, a Levite came down the road. The Levites helped the priests in the temple ceremonies. He knew what was right, but he also crossed to the other side of the street.

Then a Samaritan came. This Samaritan didn't care that the wounded man was a Jew. The good Samaritan cleaned and bandaged the man's cuts. Then he put him on his donkey and took him to an inn, which was a place where travelers could stay.

At the inn the Samaritan paid for the injured man's room and food and took care of him. When he left the next morning, he gave money to the innkeeper, making sure he had enough to help the man until he was well.

During our lives we will often meet people who are hurt—whether in their bodies or their feelings. They may look different than we do, or they may belong to a different church. It may be easiest just to walk away and not help them.

But we should help others even if no one else does. Jesus said we should love everyone, and we show our love to Heavenly Father by helping others.

•12•
The Word of Wisdom

Doctrine and Covenants 89:4, 18–21
"The Word of Wisdom" (CS, 154)

When Joseph Smith was the Prophet for the Church, many of the members were using things that were not good for their bodies. Joseph Smith was concerned about these people. He decided to pray to Heavenly Father to know what to do. The Lord answered by giving him the revelation known as the Word of Wisdom.

In the Word of Wisdom the Lord told Joseph that alcoholic beverages and hot drinks, especially coffee and tea, are not good for the body. Joseph was also told that smoking and chewing tobacco is not good for the body either.

There are some things that are very good for our bodies. The Word of Wisdom said that fruits, herbs, and vegetables are to be eaten with wisdom and thankful hearts. Wheat, rice, corn, and oats are good for us and can help us to be healthy.

The Word of Wisdom helps us to know that our bodies are a gift from our Heavenly Father. If we obey the Word of Wisdom and God's other commandments, the Lord tells us he will help us grow in gospel knowledge, he will protect us, and he will help us be healthier and stronger.

As we read in the Doctrine and Covenants, those who keep the Word of Wisdom "shall find wisdom and great treasures of knowledge, even hidden treasures; and shall run and not be weary, and shall walk and not faint" (D&C 89:19–20).

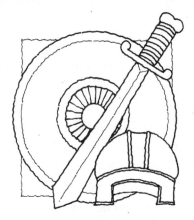

•13•
The Armor of God

Ephesians 6:11–17
"I Am a Child of God" (CS, 2)

Long ago, when soldiers went into battle, they dressed in metal armor to protect themselves. They wore helmets and breastplates, and they carried swords and shields to protect themselves from the swords and arrows of their enemies.

Once when the Nephites wore armor, the Lamanite armies retreated in fear because the Nephite army had much better protection. When they finally did fight, many more Lamanites were killed and wounded because of their lack of armor.

In our battle against evil today, we can protect

ourselves by wearing a different kind of armor. It is called the armor of God. The apostle Paul taught about this armor because there were many Roman soldiers in the land, and when the people saw them they could be reminded of how to protect themselves from evil.

The armor of God helps us to have spiritual strength. It helps us to withstand temptation and unclean things. Satan is just waiting for any opportunity to throw arrows at us. If we clothe ourselves with spiritual strength, we can know true peace and be an example of someone who puts on the whole armor of God.

The important pieces of the armor of God are: *Girdle,* or belt (of truth), *breastplate* (of righteousness), *shoes* (helping us to walk in gospel paths), *shield* (of faith), *helmet* (of salvation), *sword* (of the Spirit).

Just as the Nephite armies protected themselves in battle, so can we do things to protect ourselves when battling the adversary. If we remember to wear these pieces of armor every day of our lives, we will have protection from Satan.

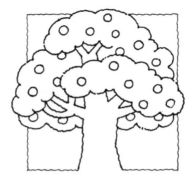

•14•
Lehi's Vision of the Tree of Life

1 Nephi 8:10-12
"The Iron Rod" (Hymns, 274)

The Lord showed the prophet Lehi a special dream or vision. In this dream, Lehi saw a beautiful tree called the tree of life. The tree was filled with delicious fruit that was exceedingly white, and when he tasted it he said it was the sweetest he had ever tasted and it filled him with joy. He was told that those who reached the tree and ate of the fruit would receive eternal life.

In the dream, Lehi wanted his family to partake of the fruit, so he called to them. Many of them came and ate the fruit with him, and he rejoiced.

Lehi saw that the only way to reach the tree of life was to hold onto a metal railing along a very narrow path. This railing was called *the iron rod.* If people didn't hold on, they would fall into a river and perish, or they would get lost in mists of darkness. Some found their way to a tall building filled with wicked people. Lehi saw many people get lost, but he also saw many people grab onto the iron rod and hold on tightly. Once these people reached the tree, they partook of the fruit and were very happy.

Later, Nephi helped us to understand the meaning of his father's dream. The tree stands for the love of God, and the fruit is the joy we feel because of Christ's sacrifice for us. The river and mists of darkness represent wickedness and the temptations of Satan. The people in the building are those who love worldly things and are ashamed of God and righteousness. The rod of iron stands for the word of God, or the guidance of God through the Holy Ghost, the prophets, and the scriptures.

If we hold to the iron rod, or in other words, listen and do what the scriptures, the prophets, and the Spirit say, we will have eternal life, which is a gift from Christ to all those who keep the commandments. And that is the greatest joy of all.

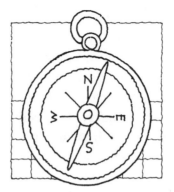

•15•
The Liahona

1 Nephi 16:10, 28-29
"Choose the Right Way" (CS, 160)

Lehi was a righteous man. He had a vision that Jerusalem, where he lived, would be destroyed because of the wickedness of the people. The Lord commanded Lehi to take his family into the wilderness where they could be safe. Later, the Lord said, he would take them to a land of promise. Lehi's family included his wife, Sariah, four sons named Laman, Lemuel, Sam, and Nephi, and several daughters.

The family went into the wilderness and set up a camp, where they waited for the Lord's guidance. One morning, Lehi found an unfamiliar object on the ground outside his tent. It was a round ball and was made of very fine brass. Attached to the ball were two little pointers, or spindles. The ball was called the Liahona. The Lord gave Lehi the Liahona to help guide his family to the promised land.

The family gathered up their belongings and continued their journey. When Lehi and his family were righteous, the Liahona pointed the way for them to go. When they complained, quarreled, and did not obey the Lord, the Liahona wouldn't work.

They hunted for food with bows and arrows while they traveled. Nephi's bow broke and his brothers' bows lost their strength, so they were unable to find food. They were all hungry, and Laman and Lemuel became angry. Nephi made a new wooden bow and asked his father where he should hunt. Lehi asked God for help, and God answered by showing the way through the Liahona. Nephi followed the instructions and found animals to feed his family.

The Liahona guided Lehi and his family through the wilderness and all the way to the promised land.

The Lord has given us a blessing like the Liahona. It is the Holy Ghost, which helps us have feelings that point the way we should go. When we are righteous, we can receive direction from the Holy Ghost, and he will help us to do the things the Lord wants us to do.

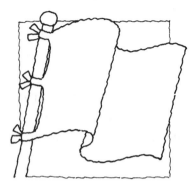

•16•
Moroni and the Title of Liberty

Alma 46:12–16

"We Are All Enlisted" (Hymns, 250)

One of the Nephites was a wicked man named Amalickiah, who wanted to be king. Many Nephites left the Church to follow him.

When Captain Moroni, the leader of the Nephite armies, heard of Amalickiah's plan to be king, he became angry. He knew that if Amalickiah became king, he would try to destroy the church of God and take away the people's liberty.

Moroni tore his coat to make a flag. On it he

wrote a message to remind the people to defend their religion, freedom, and peace. Moroni put the flag on a pole and called it the *title of liberty*. He told his people to think of their freedom and to think of their families. Then, dressed in his armor, he knelt to pray. He asked God to protect those who believed in Jesus Christ and prayed for freedom in the land, calling it a land of liberty.

Moroni went among the people. Waving the title of liberty, he called them to come and help protect their freedom. People came from all over the land. They promised to obey God's commandments and to fight for freedom.

When Amalickiah saw how many Nephites had joined with Moroni, he was afraid. Amalickiah saw that he couldn't win, so he and his people ran away. He and his followers left to join the Lamanites. Moroni and his army tried to stop them, but Amalickiah and a few of his men escaped. Moroni placed a title of liberty on every tower in the Nephite land. The Nephites had kept their freedom and again had peace.

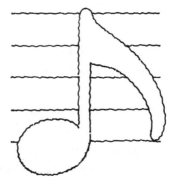

•17•
Music

Doctrine and Covenants 25:12
"Come, Come, Ye Saints" (Hymns, 30)

When the pioneers left their homes in Nauvoo and moved west, they had to travel in covered wagons or handcarts. Traveling was hard, and the pioneers were usually very tired by the end of the day.

At night the pioneers gathered their animals and wagons in a circle and built a large fire in the middle of the circle. Brigham Young, the prophet, knew the people would be happier on their journey if they had music. The pioneers who brought fiddles, trumpets, and drums used them to make music. Everyone sang and danced around the fire. The music gave the pioneers strength and courage. When they went to bed at night after singing and dancing, they felt happy.

One night a group of Latter-day Saint pioneers sang and danced around a bonfire until they were tired. Then, before going to bed in their wagons, they sang "Come, Come, Ye Saints," a song they used to encourage each other and show their dedication to the Lord.

That night a thousand unfriendly Indians were hiding around the camp, ready to attack the pioneers. But after the Indians heard the pioneers sing "Come, Come, Ye Saints," they were unable to attack. They knew the Great Spirit (their name for Heavenly Father) was watching over the pioneers, so they got on their horses and rode peacefully away.

Some time later, the man who had been chief over that group of Indians told this story to some Latter-day Saint missionaries. When he finished the story, he took out a violin and began to play "Come, Come, Ye Saints." He explained to the missionaries, "This is your song, but it is my song, too. I play it every night before I go to bed. It brings the Great Spirit here to me and makes me and my people calm and happy."

Sacred music can help us remember Heavenly Father. Singing the hymns of Zion can be just like a prayer unto him.

•18•
Daniel and His Friends

Daniel 1:11-20
"The Lord Gave Me a Temple" (CS, 153)

God sent the Jews the great blessing of having prophets like Moses and Elijah. But there came a time when the Jews did not listen to the prophets. They would not repent. God sent the king of Babylon and his army to destroy Jerusalem. They burned the homes of the people and broke down the walls around Jerusalem. Some Jews were killed and some were captured. They were taken to Babylon to be slaves.

The king also brought back to his kingdom some well-favored children of Israel. Four of these children were Daniel, Shadrach, Meshach, and Abednego. The king told his servants to feed them rich and unhealthy foods and wines. The king wanted them to eat the same foods that he would eat himself. When the food and wine were brought to them, however, they would not eat or drink it because they had been taught to eat only healthy things. They asked the king's servant to bring them food that grew from seeds and grains. They drank water, not wine. The king's servant gave them good food for ten days.

After ten days went by, the king's servant looked at Daniel and his friends. They looked better than the other children. Eventually Daniel, Shadrach, Meshach, and Abednego were taken to the king. The king told them they were wiser than his wise men. Daniel and his friends obeyed God, and God blessed them. God had made them strong and wise.

•19•
Esau and Jacob

Genesis 25:23–26; 27:37–38
"Choose the Right" (Hymns, 239)

Isaac was a son of Abraham. When his wife Rebekah was pregnant with twin boys, the Lord revealed to her that her sons would become leaders of two nations. The Lord also said that the younger son would be the leader of his brother.

These two sons were very different. The first boy, Esau, was reddish, and his body was covered with hair. The second boy, Jacob, was smoothed-skinned. Esau loved to hunt, while Jacob worked at home.

One day when they were older, Esau came in from a hunt. He asked Jacob for some soup Jacob had made. Jacob said Esau could have some soup if he would give Jacob his birthright, which included the right to lead the family. Esau was very hungry, and he did not care very much about the birthright, so he traded it for the soup. Esau made other choices that showed he did not love the Lord, while Jacob was righteous.

Years later, when Isaac was old and blind, he asked Esau to bring him some meat to eat. After he did this, Isaac said, he would bless him with the birthright. When Rebekah heard what Isaac said, she remembered what the Lord had told her about Jacob being the leader. She told Jacob to pretend to be Esau so he could receive the blessing.

While Esau was hunting for meat, Jacob dressed like Esau and took some goat meat to his father. Isaac thought Jacob was Esau, and he blessed him with the birthright. He blessed Jacob that people would serve him and that he would rule over his brother and other nations.

When Esau had found out what happened, he wept. He had lost the blessings that could have been his because he had not lived worthy of them.

•20•
Latter-day Prophets

Doctrine and Covenants 1:38
"Follow the Prophet" (CS, 110, esp. v. 9)

As members of The Church of Jesus Christ of Latter-day Saints, we are so blessed to have a living prophet on the earth to lead us. The prophet teaches us things that our Heavenly Father wants us to know. He warns us about what will happen if we do not follow the commandments. He also tells us of the wonderful blessings that will come when we do obey.

The prophet is the president of the Church. He is chosen of God and called through priesthood authority. He listens to God's voice and obeys Him in all things.

When a prophet dies, the Church does not hold an election to choose the next prophet. Instead, the apostles meet to learn from the Lord who he wants to serve the Church as prophet. There have been fourteen prophets since Joseph Smith who have served us and our Heavenly Father.

Because our Heavenly Father loves us, he has sent us a prophet to teach and guide us today. The Lord has promised us that the prophet will never lead the Church astray. If we listen and follow the prophet, our lives will be happier, we will be safer, and one day we will return and live with our Heavenly Father.

•21•
The Widow's Mite

Mark 12:41–44

"Because I Have Been Given Much" (Hymns, 219)

Once when Jesus was in Jerusalem at the temple, he watched while people put large amounts of money into the treasury. The treasury was a container on the temple grounds where people could give money to help with the work of the temple.

Jesus then saw a poor widow, whose husband had died, put two mites into this box. Two mites was not very much money. In fact, today it would be worth less than a penny. But even though she didn't have much to give, she gave all she had.

Jesus then called his disciples to gather around

him, and he told them what he had seen. He told them about the rich men who had given lots of money. And he told them about the widow. The rich people didn't give everything they had; they still had a lot of money left after they made their donation. But the widow sacrificed everything. Because of that, Jesus taught, the widow gave more than all of the rich people, even though she gave only two mites.

Jesus taught us that how much we give is not the most important thing. What matters most is that we want to do all we can to help God's work on this earth.

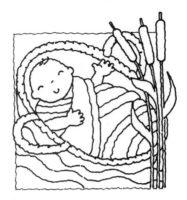

•22•
Baby Moses

Exodus 2:2-10
"I Feel My Savior's Love" (CS, 74)

The Israelites are the main group of people we read about in the Bible. Once when there was a famine in their land, the Lord helped them find food in Egypt, so they all moved there. After they had lived in Egypt for a long time, the king, who was called the pharaoh, became afraid of them. He thought there were too many of them and decided that all the Israelite baby boys must be killed. He sent people to kill any baby boys who were born.

When one Israelite mother had a baby boy, she hid him for three months to keep him safe. But he was growing bigger, and she knew she could not hide him much longer. She was a wise woman who loved and trusted in the Lord. She wove a basket and covered it with tar so no water would get in. She then put her sweet baby boy in the basket. She put the basket in the tall grass by the river. The baby's sister stood by to watch the baby.

The pharaoh's daughter saw the basket and opened it. The baby began to cry. The pharaoh's daughter felt sorry for the baby and wanted to take care of him, even though she knew he was an Israelite baby boy.

When the baby's sister saw what was happening, she went to the pharaoh's daughter. "Would you like me to find an Israelite woman to help take care of this baby for you?" she asked. The pharaoh's daughter agreed. Then the baby's sister ran and got her mother so she could take care of her own son. The pharaoh's daughter named him Moses.

When he grew up, Moses became the ruler of the Israelite people. He became a mighty prophet of God and was able to lead his people away from the wicked pharaoh.

•23•
Let Your Light Shine

Matthew 5:14–16
"I Am Like a Star" (CS, 163)

Jesus Christ taught those who followed him that they were the light of the world. He said that you don't light candles and put them under baskets. When you light a candle, you put it on a candlestick so that it gives light to everyone in the room. He told us, "Let your light so shine before men, that they may see your good works, and glorify your Father which is in heaven."

That means that if you are a good example, you will be letting your light shine. Then when other people see your good example, they will know that you love Heavenly Father, and they, too, will want to honor him.

We can let our light shine by keeping the commandments and choosing the right. When we are honest, when we keep the Sabbath holy, and when we are kind, we are letting our light shine. When we obey the Word of Wisdom, when we dress modestly, and when we use the names of Heavenly Father and Jesus Christ reverently, we are letting our light shine. When we share our testimonies with others, we are letting our light shine.

We can be a good example just like Jesus. He was a good example for us and showed us the things we need to do to be happy and to be able to return to live with our Heavenly Father. No matter how young or old we are, we must always let our light shine so that all may see.

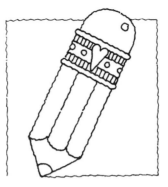

•24•
Journal Writing

2 Nephi 25:26

"Keep the Commandments" (Hymns, 303)

The scriptures are the most important books in the world. They are filled with important messages to us from our Heavenly Father. When we read the scriptures, we learn about people who lived many years ago and how they learned to follow God.

The scriptures tell us that many people of long ago were commanded to keep a record of their lives. If they had not obeyed, we wouldn't have the scriptures today. When Jesus visited the Nephites, he chastised those who failed to record spiritual events.

We should also keep records of our lives. Today

many people call this type of record a journal. In a journal we can write about many things. Tell about your feelings, what you think about, and what makes you happy or sad. It is not necessary to write every day, but you should write in your journal often. Sundays are a good time to write. President Spencer W. Kimball said, "Those who keep a personal journal are more likely to keep the Lord in remembrance in their daily lives."*

One important reason to write in a journal is that the prophets have asked us to. Another reason is to help us understand and learn about ourselves. A third important reason to keep a journal is to record how you are progressing spiritually.

Keeping a journal will help to remind you of the blessings of our Heavenly Father. Bearing your testimony on paper will help it to grow, and it will strengthen others who read it later on.

---

*"President Kimball Speaks Out on Personal Journals," *New Era*, December 1980, 27.

•25•
Honesty

Article of Faith 13
"I Believe in Being Honest" (CS, 149)

Heavenly Father wants us to be honest and truthful at all times and in all places. It is not always easy. If you do something wrong, you might be ashamed or afraid to admit it. But when you are honest about your mistakes, you can repent and be forgiven.

Even when you have not done anything wrong, sometimes it is hard to stand up for what is right. It can take real courage to stand up for the truth. It is not always easy to express your testimony of Heavenly Father and his Son, Jesus Christ. But when you are honest about your feelings and your testimony, the Holy Ghost will help you.

As a young man, Joseph F. Smith was on a journey with a small group of Latter-day Saints. As they set up camp one evening, some drunken men rode up on horseback and threatened to kill any Mormons they found. Some of the Saints hid in the bushes by the creek.

Joseph F. Smith, who had been gathering wood, boldly approached the fire. One of the drunken men, pointing his pistol at Joseph, said he planned to kill every Mormon he met. "Are you a 'Mormon'?" he demanded. Without a pause, Joseph F. Smith looked the ruffian in the eye and answered, "Yes, siree, dyed in the wool, true blue, through and through."

The man was so surprised by Joseph's honest answer that he grabbed Joseph's hand and said, "Well, you are the _____ _____ pleasantest man I ever met! Shake, young fellow, I am glad to see a man that stands up for his convictions." The drunken men then rode off and did not bother the Saints again.*

You can be like Joseph F. Smith. You can be honest and truthful at all times and in all places. Decide ahead of time that you will always be honest, and Heavenly Father will bless you.

---

*Joseph Fielding Smith, *Life of Joseph F. Smith* (Salt Lake City: Deseret Book, 1938), 189.

•26•
The Golden Rule

Matthew 7:12

"Love One Another" (CS, 136)

One of the things Jesus taught during the Sermon on the Mount is called the Golden Rule. The Golden Rule says, "Do unto others as you would have others do unto you." In other words, we should treat people the way we want to be treated. We should treat them with respect, kindness, and love. We should help others when they are in need. We should pray for other people, including those who might be rude or unkind to us.

Just think how wonderful the world would be if everyone practiced the Golden Rule. There wouldn't be any more fighting or war. People wouldn't be mean or rude to each other. They wouldn't call names or hit others. There wouldn't be any more crime. People wouldn't steal or lie or cheat. Marriages would be stronger and families would be happier. The world would be a wonderful place if we would just live that one commandment.

We can learn to become kind and loving by doing kind and loving things. We can also pray for the Lord to help us to live the Golden Rule. If we pray sincerely, he will bless us to do better, and we will gradually become more and more like him.

President Gordon B. Hinckley has taught, "God is the father of our spirits. . . . We are all brothers and sisters and we ought to treat one another as brothers and sisters, with kindness and respect and love, with an implementation of the golden rule."*

---

*Teachings of Gordon B. Hinckley (Salt Lake City: Deseret Book, 1997), 667–68.

•27•
Ammon and the King

Alma 18:7-10

"I Will Be Valiant" (CS, 162)

Ammon was one of the four sons of Mosiah. When the Lord commanded Ammon and his brothers to teach the Lamanites the gospel, the brothers all separated and went to different cities. Ammon went to the city of Ishmael.

The Lamanites did not like the Nephites. They tied up Ammon and took him to their king, whose name was Lamoni. He asked Ammon why he had come to his city. Ammon said he wanted to live with the Lamanites. He wanted to be the king's servant.

King Lamoni liked Ammon and gave him the job of tending the king's sheep.

One day while the sheep were drinking water, some wicked Lamanites came and scattered the sheep. They wanted to steal the sheep. The king's servants were afraid the king would kill them because the sheep were gone. But Ammon helped them find the sheep again.

Later, the wicked Lamanites came again to steal the sheep. Ammon went to fight the wicked Lamanites. The Lamanites thought they could kill Ammon, but Ammon had the power of God with him. He threw stones with his sling and killed some of the wicked Lamanites. Then the Lamanites tried to kill Ammon with their clubs, but he cut off their arms. The wicked men became afraid and ran away.

When the king learned what had happened he wanted to see Ammon, but he was afraid of him. Ammon went to the king and told him he was a servant of God. King Lamoni asked Ammon to teach him, and Ammon taught the king about God and Jesus Christ.

When King Lamoni heard Ammon's teachings, he believed Ammon, and he became a member of the Lord's true Church. Many of his people joined the Church as well.

•28•
Tithing

Doctrine and Covenants 119:3–4
"I'm Glad to Pay a Tithing" (CS, 150)

When the Church was just beginning, the Lord told Joseph Smith and the Saints that they should pay tithing. Later the Lord revealed that tithing should be one-tenth of all their income. If a person earns ten cents, one penny should be paid for tithing. And if a person earns one hundred dollars, he or she should give ten dollars for tithing.

Our Heavenly Father and Jesus have given us everything we have. In return, they've asked that we pay tithing each time we earn or receive money. Paying tithing is one way we can show our faith and love to Heavenly Father and Jesus. When we do, we will receive even more blessings.

Tithing money is used to build temples and meetinghouses, to help with missionary work, and to do many other important things. When members pay tithing, they give it to the bishop or branch president. Then he sends it to Church headquarters, where Church leaders decide how the tithing should be used.

Heavenly Father promised wonderful blessings to those who pay their tithing. Those who do not pay tithing do not receive the same blessings as those who do. The Bible says that people who do not pay tithing are robbing God, for everything belongs to him.

President Joseph F. Smith said that through tithing "the loyalty of the people of this Church shall be put to the test. By this principle it shall be known who is for the kingdom of God and who is against it. By this principle it shall be seen whose hearts are set on doing the will of God and keeping his commandments. . . . By it shall be known whether we are faithful or unfaithful."*

---

*Joseph F. Smith, *Gospel Doctrine* (Salt Lake City: Deseret Book, 1939), 225.

•29•
Family Garden

Doctrine and Covenants 6:33
"The Prophet Said to Plant a Garden" (CS, 237)

President Spencer W. Kimball said: "We encourage you to grow all the food that you feasibly can on your own property. Berry bushes, grapevines, fruit trees—plant them if your climate is right for their growth. Grow vegetables and eat them from your own yard. Even those residing in apartments or condominiums can generally grow a little food in pots and planters. Study the best methods of providing your own foods. Make your garden neat and attractive as well as productive. If there are children in your home, involve them in the process with assigned responsibilities."*

Gardens can be very helpful to families. Gardening teaches the gardener the law of the harvest, showing us that we reap what we sow and nurture. It helps us appreciate and love nature. It teaches families to work together. When we have gardens, we are able to be more self-sufficient, so we do not have to depend on others so much for food. Having a garden helps families plan nutritious meals. It can help us to save money and help others in need.

If our families follow the counsel of our prophets to have a garden, our hard work will continue to bring a more abundant harvest each year. The Lord has promised to provide us with abundance if we live his commandments.

---

*"Family Preparedness," *Ensign,* May 1976, 124.

•30•
The Wise Man and the Foolish Man

Matthew 7:24-27

"The Wise Man and the Foolish Man" (CS, 281)

Heavenly Father has a plan for this earth. In his plan, every person who lives on this earth is given the power to choose how he or she will live. Will we choose to live wisely, or will we choose foolishly?

In one of Jesus' sermons he talked about this choice. He told the people the right way to live, and then he taught them that living their lives was like building a house. If we choose to live as Christ taught, we are like a man who built his house on rock. If we choose to disobey Christ, we are like a man who built his house on sand.

If we build our house on a solid foundation, it will never fall or crumble. But if we choose to build our house on sand, when the rains and storms come our testimony will be destroyed.

One way we can build the house of our lives on rock is to gain a testimony of Jesus Christ. We must build our testimonies on the basic truths of the gospel, like baptism, prayer, church attendance, and righteousness. We must do the things Jesus asked us to do in the Sermon on the Mount: be humble and pure, be a peacemaker, be an example for others, love our neighbors (and our enemies too!), pray to Heavenly Father each day, and do the things he asks us to do.

There will be times in our lives when we will experience floods, storms, and trials. We will be tested. The only way we will make it through these storms is if we have a strong testimony and if we remember Jesus Christ and follow him. Jesus and his teachings are our only sure foundation.

We can show that we have a testimony and faith by choosing the right each day. If we do, we will be like the wise man—building our lives upon the solid foundation of the gospel and preparing ourselves to live again with Heavenly Father and Jesus Christ.

•31•
Family History

Doctrine and Covenants 128:15
"Family History—I Am Doing It" (CS, 94)

The study of the history of families is called genealogy. When we learn our genealogy, we learn who our grandparents were, and who their parents and grandparents were, and so on.

The Lord has commanded us to search for our ancestors, find out who they are, and learn all we can about them. After we find the name of an ancestor, we can try to discover other things about him or her to help us see that individual not just as a name but as a real person.

We do genealogy because we love our ancestors

and want them to have the same gospel blessings we enjoy. Once we find records that help us identify our ancestors, we can perform ordinances for them that they may not have been able to receive for themselves while on this earth. These ordinances are performed in the temple.

Genealogy is an activity that can involve the whole family. It should involve children, youth, and parents.

When you work on genealogy you may start by working on a family tree. Like a tree, you get your life and strength from your roots. Your roots are your ancestors, like your grandparents and great-grandparents, who have lived before you. A tree knows where its roots are and is always gaining strength and support from them. Our ancestors love us and we can learn much from their lives. We need to follow the counsel to work on our genealogy so that we may gain support and learn from those who have lived before us.

•32•
Rebekah at the Well

Genesis 24:10–21, 27
"I Know My Father Lives" (CS, 5)

Abraham and his family lived in a land called Canaan. He was a great and righteous follower of the Lord. Abraham's son Isaac was old enough to get married, but Abraham told Isaac that he should not marry a woman from Canaan. Abraham wanted his son to marry a young woman who also would love the Lord and be faithful in keeping his commandments. So Abraham asked his servant to go to the place where he was from and find a wife for his son there.

The servant took ten camels and went to a well outside the city of Nahor in the land of Mesopotamia.

There the servant prayed to Heavenly Father to send the woman who should be the wife of Isaac. He said in his prayer that he planned to ask one of the women who came to the well to give him a drink of water. He prayed that she would also offer a drink to his camels. If she did, that would help him to know that she was the right one.

A woman named Rebekah came to the well and did just as the servant had prayed someone would. She was the answer to his prayers.

When Rebekah's family heard what had happened, they believed it was God's will. Though she had not met Isaac, Rebekah trusted in the Lord and knew that he had guided the servant to her. With faith, she agreed to go with the servant and become Isaac's wife. Through her obedience to the Lord, Rebekah was a great influence for good in the life of her husband and her family.

•33•
Daniel and the Lions' Den

Daniel 6:16–23

"A Prayer Song" (CS, 22)

Daniel was a faithful Israelite man living in the land of Babylon. He was one of the main rulers of the land, helping the king, Darius.

Some of the other rulers were jealous of Daniel, and they wanted to have his power. They plotted together to get rid of him. They convinced King Darius to sign a law saying that no one could pray to God. They knew that Daniel prayed faithfully, and that he would break the law. The law said that all those who did not obey the law would be put into the lions' den, and the lions would eat them.

Daniel was still obedient to God and prayed three times a day. Those wanting to kill Daniel spied on his house, and when they saw him praying, they hurried to tell the king. King Darius loved Daniel and realized he had been tricked. The king tried to change the law to save Daniel, but he was reminded that no law could be changed. King Darius knew that Daniel had to be put in the lions' den.

When evening came, Daniel was thrown into the den of hungry lions. The king told Daniel that he knew God would save him. The king fasted all night. He was so worried he could not sleep. Early the next morning he hurried to the lions' den and called out to Daniel, and Daniel answered. The lions had not hurt him. He did not suffer even one scratch from the lions. God had sent an angel to shut the mouths of the lions.

King Darius was very happy because God had helped Daniel. The king commanded that all the wicked rulers were to be put in the lions' den, where they were killed at once. He also commanded that his entire kingdom worship the true and living God whom Daniel worshiped.

•34•
The Holy Ghost

Mark 1:9–11
"The Holy Ghost" (CS, 105)

John the Baptist taught people about the Savior and testified that he would be coming soon. He taught the people to repent and that they needed to be baptized to wash away their sins. He also taught them that Jesus would come and give them the gift of the Holy Ghost.

One day Jesus sought out John, who was baptizing people in the Jordan River, and asked him to baptize him. John knew that the Savior was sinless and did not need to be baptized to wash away his sins. But Jesus told him that Heavenly Father had commanded all people to be baptized. John the Baptist agreed, and went down into the water with Jesus to baptize him. When Jesus came out of the water, Heavenly Father's voice was heard saying, "This is my beloved Son, in whom I am well pleased" (Matthew 3:17). The heavens then opened up, "and the Holy Ghost descended in a bodily shape like a dove upon him" (Luke 3:22).

After we are baptized and confirmed members of The Church of Jesus Christ of Latter-day Saints, if we are worthy we can receive the gift of the Holy Ghost just as Jesus did. The Holy Ghost will be our companion and comforter. He will give us guidance and direction in our lives. He is our guardian of peace and happiness. He can warn us of danger and can help to keep us from making mistakes. He will help us to be happy. The Holy Ghost can be with us twenty-four hours a day.

Elder Robert D. Hales said, "The right to His constant companionship is among the greatest gifts we can receive in mortality, for by the light of His promptings and His cleansing power, we can be led back into the presence of God."* If we are worthy the Holy Ghost will be our constant companion and help us to be more righteous.

---

*"Out of Darkness into His Marvelous Light," *Ensign,* May 2002, 70.

•35•
Noah and the Ark

Genesis 6:12–14, 17–22
"We Listen to a Prophet's Voice" (Hymns, 22)

Noah was a prophet long ago when the world was extremely wicked. The prophets told the people to repent, but they would not listen. Instead, they became even more wicked.

Because Noah was a righteous man he found favor with the Lord. The Lord told him He was going to clean the earth of its wickedness by sending a great flood. He instructed Noah to build a giant boat, called an ark, which would protect Noah and his family from the flood. Noah was told that he would bring two of every kind of animal, male and female, into the ark to keep them alive. He was also told to store food for his family and for the animals.

The Lord told Noah to warn the wicked people that if they did not repent and live righteously, He would make it rain for forty days and forty nights until the entire earth was flooded. The wicked people laughed at Noah and thought he was crazy to build an ark.

Noah followed the instruction of the Lord. When the ark was finished, he and his family shut the door. Torrents of rain fell upon the earth for forty days and forty nights. The flood continued upon the earth until the ark began to float. Every living thing that was upon the earth was destroyed except for Noah's family and the animals that they had gathered. After another one hundred and fifty days the waters began to dry up.

When the land was dry, Noah was commanded to leave the ark and settle upon the land. Noah built an altar unto Heavenly Father to thank him for keeping his family safe.

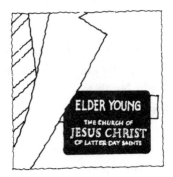

•36•
Alma the Younger

Mosiah 27:8-37

"I Hope They Call Me on a Mission" (CS, 169)

In the Book of Mormon we read of a prophet by the name of Alma and a king named Mosiah. They were very righteous men and did their best to help the people and teach them the gospel. But King Mosiah's sons and a son of Alma called Alma the Younger did not believe in the Church and would not listen to their fathers. These sons were very wicked men who led many others away from the Church.

The Lord loved Alma the Younger and his friends, but he did not like the things they were doing. As they were going about rebelling against God, the

Lord sent an angel to them. The angel appeared and spoke with a voice of thunder, shaking the earth on which they stood. Alma the Younger and the sons of Mosiah were so astonished that they fell to the ground.

The angel said, "Alma, . . . why persecutest thou the church of God? For the Lord hath said: This is my church, and I will establish it; and nothing shall overthrow it, save it is the transgression of my people" (Mosiah 27:13).

After the angel left, Alma was so weak that he could not move his hands or legs, and he could not speak. The sons of Mosiah took Alma the Younger to his father, Alma the prophet, who fasted and prayed for him. After two days had passed, Alma the Younger received strength and stood up and began to speak of what happened to them. He told his father he had repented of his sins and had been forgiven by Heavenly Father.

From that time forward, Alma the Younger and the sons of Mosiah became great missionaries for the Lord and baptized many people into the Church.

Serving a mission like Alma and his friends did is a wonderful way to show Heavenly Father that you love him and that you want to follow his commandments.

•37•
Samuel Predicts Christ's Birth

Helaman 14:2-8
"Samuel Tells of the Baby Jesus" (CS, 36)

There were times in the Book of Mormon when the Lamanites were more righteous than the Nephites. One Lamanite was a prophet named Samuel, who preached repentance to the wicked Nephite people. The Nephites rejected him and cast him out of their cities. But the Lord commanded him to return, which he did.

Five years before Christ was born, Samuel prophesied that Christ would soon come into the world and that there would be signs of his birth. He said, "Behold, there shall be great lights in heaven, insomuch that in the night before he cometh there shall be no darkness, insomuch that it shall appear unto man as if it was day. Therefore, there shall be one day and a night and a day, as if it were one day and there were no night; and this shall be unto you for a sign" (Helaman 14:3–4).

Five years later the wicked people who did not believe in Christ said that unless the prophesied sign came, they would put to death all those who believed in Christ. A righteous prophet named Nephi was deeply troubled because of their threats and prayed in behalf of the righteous believers. The voice of the Lord came to him and said, "Lift up your head and be of good cheer; for behold, the time is at hand, and on this night shall the sign be given, and on the morrow come I into the world" (3 Nephi 1:13).

When the sun went down that night there was no darkness, as if it was day, just like Samuel had prophesied. Samuel the Lamanite was a wonderful prophet who taught with great courage and power about the coming birth of Christ.

•38•
Eternal Families

Doctrine and Covenants 132:19–20
"Families Can Be Together Forever" (CS, 188)

Before we were born on this earth, we all lived together as brothers and sisters in a beautiful spirit world. We were part of a heavenly family with loving Heavenly Parents.

When we come to earth, Heavenly Father sends us into families. He loves all children and has told all parents to teach their children the gospel. When we die and leave this earth, Heavenly Father and Jesus Christ want us to live again as families in heaven. They have shown us the way for this to happen. Heavenly Father has given us a plan that allows families to be together forever.

In the temple, a husband and wife can receive an ordinance that helps them be together forever. This is called a sealing or a temple marriage. This seals them together as an eternal couple, and if they later have children, the children are automatically sealed to them when they are born. But each person has to be righteous to receive the promised blessing.

The special blessing of forever families is given only to those who are sealed in the temple and keep the promises they make there. If a couple is married outside the temple, they can later go to the temple to be sealed so they can remain married for eternity. Their children can be sealed to them and become part of their family forever.

Because Heavenly Father loves us, he wants all of his children to have the blessings that are given in the temple. There are many temples throughout the world, so righteous people around the world can have these blessings. Each of us needs to live worthy so that when we are married we can go to the temple to be sealed and start an eternal family of our own.

The temple helps us learn more about Heavenly Father and Jesus Christ and why we are here on earth. And temple ordinances like sealings make it possible for our families to be together.

•39•
Gratitude

Psalm 105:1

"Thanks to Our Father" (CS, 20)

Gratitude is appreciating the blessings that Heavenly Father gives to us. He has given us many things we can be thankful for. The world itself is a truly wonderful place, with its plants, animals, sky, stars, colors, and smells. We have food to eat and water to drink and air to breathe. We have a place to live and clothes to wear. We have family and friends.

We also have many blessings through the gospel of Jesus Christ, including scriptures, prophets, the priesthood, ordinances, sacrament meetings, temples, and Church buildings. If we seek to live righteously, we can have the help of the Holy Ghost. We have the atonement of Christ, which enables us to repent, to overcome weaknesses, and to be resurrected from the dead, so we can live forever with our Father in Heaven if we will be worthy.

We have been commanded by the Lord to be thankful for all things. We should have grateful hearts throughout our lives and cherish all the blessings that our Heavenly Father has given us. We need to recognize that our Heavenly Father has a hand in all things.

President David O. McKay said, "Gratitude is deeper than thanks. Thankfulness may consist merely of words. Gratitude is shown in acts."*

There are many ways to show gratitude to our Heavenly Father. We can show it by speaking of it in our prayers. We can show it by praying often, by honoring and worshiping him, by obeying his commandments, and by serving him. These words and deeds show our Heavenly Father that we are full of gratitude and that we love him. When we learn to show gratitude we actually become happier, and we begin to feel more peace in our lives.

---

*"Gratitude Quotations," *Friend,* November 1975, 39.

•40•
Feeding Thousands

Mark 6:34-44

"Come, Ye Thankful People" (Hymns, 94)

One day Jesus was teaching a huge crowd of people, who had come from many cities to hear him. All together there were five thousand men, along with women and children. As the day began to close, the disciples went to Jesus, concerned. They noted that it was getting late and the people didn't have any food to eat. They suggested that Jesus "send them away, that they may go into the country round about, and into the villages, and buy themselves bread" (Mark 6:36).

But Jesus had another idea. He asked the disciples to find out how much food there was among the people. They checked and came back with their report, saying that one boy had five loaves and two fishes.

Jesus told the people to sit in small groups on the grass. Then he "looked up to heaven, and blessed, and brake the loaves, and gave them to his disciples to set before them; and the two fishes divided he among them all" (Mark 6:41).

Then a marvelous thing happened. The disciples took the food and passed it out to the people. One by one the people took a portion of food, until everyone had some. The scripture says, "And they did all eat, and were filled" (Mark 6:42). No one went away hungry.

But that wasn't all. After everyone had eaten as much as they wanted, the disciples took twelve baskets to gather up what was left over. They were able to fill the baskets with the leftover bread and fish. It was a wonderful miracle.

Jesus had power to turn a little bit of food into a lot. In the same way, he can help us with the things we need. When we struggle in our lives and need help from God, it is a blessing to know that he is good and generous—and that he will give us what we need, and more besides.

•41•
Faith

Alma 32:21, 26–31
"Faith" (CS, 96)

We have faith when we believe and trust in something that is real and true even though we have not seen it for ourselves. We need to have faith in Jesus Christ. Even though we have never seen him, we know and believe that he lives. And we do the things he wants us to do.

In the Book of Mormon, Alma tells us that the word of God is like a seed. We show faith when we plant a seed in the earth. Even though we do not see the plant, we have faith that it will grow. We give it water and make sure it has sunshine. If it is a good seed, it will begin to grow.

When we learn things in the gospel, we can treat them like that seed. For the seed of the gospel to grow, we must pray, listen to the prophets, and keep the commandments. As we do this, we will see the results. We will have a good feeling inside about what we are doing, and the seeds of truth will grow in our hearts. All this is part of exercising faith in our lives. Throughout our lives, we need to nourish our faith with diligence and patience, and we will feel it grow.

Alma said that if we always nourish the word of God by our faith, it will grow as large as a tree and will bring forth good fruit. Our faith in Jesus Christ will then grow strong and bring blessings for us and others we serve.

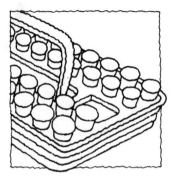

•42•
The Sacrament

Doctrine and Covenants 20:77, 79
"The Sacrament" (CS, 72)

Near the end of his life, Jesus gathered his apostles around him to share a special meal with them. He knew that the time for his great sacrifice had come, that his blood would be shed and that his body would die. To help his apostles remember him, Jesus took some bread, blessed it, broke it, and gave it to them, saying, "Take, eat; this is in remembrance of my body which I give a ransom for you" (JST Matthew 26:22).

He then took a cup, gave thanks, and gave it to them, saying, "Drink ye all of it" (JST Matthew 26:23). He explained, "This is in remembrance of my blood . . . , which is shed for as many as shall believe on my name, for the remission of their sins" (JST Matthew 26:24).

Jesus' apostles partook of the sacrament and later taught the other disciples about this new ordinance.

We have also been taught and commanded to participate in this same ordinance. We partake of the sacrament, just as Jesus' apostles did, in remembrance of his body and blood. When we take the sacrament, we should think about his life and his sacrifice for us.

We have the opportunity to attend sacrament meeting each week. Sunday is the most important day of the week, and sacrament meeting is the most important meeting of the week. The Lord has commanded us to attend sacrament meeting. During sacrament meeting, we have the privilege to partake of the sacrament and remember him.

When we are baptized, we make a covenant with our Heavenly Father. Part of the covenant is to be part of Jesus' family, to follow him, and to remember him. Each time we listen to the sacrament prayers and partake of the sacrament, we are renewing that covenant with our Heavenly Father.

•43•
The Brother of Jared

Ether 3:4–13
"Beautiful Savior" (CS, 62)

Jared and his brother were very righteous, but they lived at a time of great wickedness. When they sought the Lord for guidance, the Lord told them he desired to send them to a land of promise. That land is now called America.

The brother of Jared gathered his family and his friends. They took their flocks, birds, fish, honeybees, and seeds of every kind. After they had traveled for four years, the Lord came in a cloud and talked to the brother of Jared for three hours. The Lord chastised him for not praying. The brother of Jared repented and prayed to the Lord. The Lord then forgave him and his brethren of their sins and commanded them not to sin again.

The Lord told the brother of Jared to build eight boats like submarines for their journey to the promised land. The Lord gave them instructions to make the boats small and light. After the boats were finished, the brother of Jared went to the Lord with a problem. There would be no light in the barges and they would not be able to see. The brother of Jared asked the Lord what they should do to light up the inside of the boats.

The Lord answered by asking him to think of a solution. So the brother of Jared melted sixteen small stones from a big rock. He asked Jesus to touch the stones with his finger to make them shine. Jesus answered his prayer by reaching down and touching each stone with his finger.

Because of his great faith, the brother of Jared saw the finger of the Lord as he touched the stones. The Lord then blessed him by showing him his whole spirit body, teaching him that all men are created in the Lord's image.

They put the stones into the barges and sailed toward the promised land. They traveled for 344 days. When they reached the promised land, the first thing they did was offer a prayer of thanksgiving.

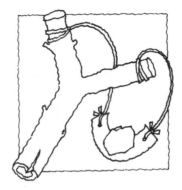

•44•
David and Goliath

1 Samuel 17:45-50
"Dare to Do Right" (CS, 158)

The Philistines were enemies of the children of Israel, and the two nations went to war. One of the greatest warriors for the Philistines was a giant named Goliath. Goliath was over nine feet tall. Goliath challenged the Israelites to choose one of their men to fight him. Whoever won the fight would win the war for his nation. The men of the armies of Israel were afraid of Goliath, and they fled. None of the Israelites wanted to fight him.

David was a young man who had three older brothers in the Israelite army. David's father sent him to take some food to his brothers, who were at war.

While David was visiting his brothers, he saw Goliath and heard him shouting. He knew that the men were afraid of Goliath and said that he would go to fight the giant. His oldest brother was angry when he heard that. David should be home taking care of the sheep, he said. But David felt he should try to fight Goliath. He knew God would help him.

He picked up five smooth stones and put them in his pouch. Then he took his sling and went to fight Goliath. When Goliath saw how young and small David was, he made fun of David. David answered that God would help him kill Goliath.

Goliath had a long sword and had armor on his body. David didn't wear any armor and didn't have a sword. David just had his sling and rocks. When Goliath came at David to kill him, David put a stone in his sling and threw the stone. The stone hit Goliath in the forehead, and he fell on his face. David took Goliath's sword and cut his head off.

When the Philistines saw that their champion was dead, they ran. King Saul, the king of the Israelites, honored David by making him the leader of his armies. Because of David's courage, and his faith in our Heavenly Father, he was able to overcome Goliath.

•45•
Protecting God's Creations

Genesis 2:8–9, 15
"All Things Bright and Beautiful" (CS, 231)

The heaven (including the sun, moon, and stars) and the earth were created by Jesus Christ under the direction of Heavenly Father. Heavenly Father and Jesus Christ created Adam and Eve, the first man and woman on the earth, and placed them in a beautiful garden called Eden. Adam was commanded to take care of the garden and to name "every living creature" (Genesis 2:19).

You are part of Adam's family, and you, too, can

help care for the earth. You can plant a flower, a tree, or a garden to make the earth more beautiful. Besides beauty, plants also provide oxygen, food, and shelter. You can help save water and food by not using more than you need.

You can care for the animals by being kind to them and providing food and shelter for them. They are our friends and helpers, given to us for our benefit and use and to gladden our hearts. Some help us work, some give us food, some give us fiber for clothing, and many give us affection and companionship as pets.

Heavenly Father gave us plants, flowers, and animals for our enjoyment. We need to thank Heavenly Father for all the beautiful creatures he has put on the earth and remember that we were commanded by Heavenly Father to take care of them and protect them. When we care for the plants and animals of the earth, we are showing our gratitude and reverence for these wonderful creations.

•46•
Stripling Warriors

Alma 56:45-48, 55-56
"We'll Bring the World His Truth" (CS, 172)

The Lamanites and Nephites had many wars. The Nephites fought hard to protect themselves and their families. They also fought to protect the people of Ammon, who had promised God they would not shed any blood. As the Nephites fought, the people of Ammon saw that the armies needed help. They wanted to help fight for their country, but Helaman, a son of Alma the Younger, told them to keep their promise.

The people of Ammon had many young sons who were strong, brave, and righteous. These sons had not promised God that they would not fight. These two thousand sons met together and promised that they would fight for and help protect their country. Their mothers taught them to be righteous and have faith in God, so they were not afraid to fight. They asked Helaman to be their leader.

When Helaman led the young warriors to the place of battle, they came upon the Nephites and Lamanites fighting. The Lamanites were winning. Helaman's army helped the Nephites. Helaman gave orders and the young men obeyed and fought bravely. At the end of the fight, the Nephites, with help of the young stripling warriors, had won.

After the battle, one thousand Nephite soldiers were dead, and Helaman was afraid many of his young men had also been killed. But not one of them died. They had faith that God would help and bless them, and he did.

The two thousand stripling warriors had to be righteous and work together to have Heavenly Father protect them. The Nephites knew that Heavenly Father had blessed them because they had listened to the teachings of their mothers. We must always have faith and live righteously so that we may receive all the blessings our Heavenly Father desires to give us.

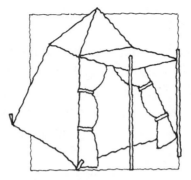

•47•
Lehi's Journey

1 Nephi 1:4–7
"Nephi's Courage" (CS, 120)

Lehi and his family lived in the land of Jerusalem six hundred years before Jesus Christ was born. Lehi's wife was Sariah, and they had four sons when they lived in Jerusalem: Laman, Lemuel, Sam, and Nephi. Other sons were born later. The people in Jerusalem were very wicked. God sent prophets to tell the wicked people to repent, but they would not listen.

One night Lehi had a vision. God told Lehi that Jerusalem would be destroyed. Lehi went out and began to tell the people to repent, telling them about his vision. But the wicked people didn't believe him and became very angry. Some even tried to kill him. Since the people would not listen, God spoke to Lehi in a dream and told him to leave Jerusalem before the people tried to kill him again.

Lehi and his family obeyed God and went into the wilderness. They left behind their house, their riches, most of their clothes, and all their friends. Laman and Lemuel didn't want to leave Jerusalem, but Nephi and Sam obeyed Lehi, for they believed what he had told them.

After three days, they came to a river and put up their tents. Lehi built an altar of stones and thanked God for helping them. He knew that the Lord was guiding them and that he would help them through the many trials in the desert.

Sometimes the Lord asks us to do difficult things. We may have to sacrifice things we like very much in order to please the Lord and to serve him. If we will follow the things the Lord asks of us, he will support us in our trials and help us in the challenges in our lives.

Here is the testimony Nephi bore about this wonderful truth: "If it so be that the children of men keep the commandments of God he doth nourish them, and strengthen them, and provide means whereby they can accomplish the thing which he has commanded them" (1 Nephi 17:3).

•48•
Keeping the Sabbath Day Holy

Doctrine and Covenants 59:9–13
"Remember the Sabbath Day" (CS, 155)

From the beginning, God has instructed prophets to teach his people to honor the Sabbath day. God rested from his labors on the seventh day, and this day was blessed and sanctified as a holy day. The fourth commandment to Moses was to "remember the sabbath day, to keep it holy" (Exodus 20:8).

The Sabbath is a special day. It is holy to Heavenly Father, and it should be holy to us. We should do only those things on the Sabbath that help us feel close to Heavenly Father and Jesus Christ.

We can do many good things on the Sabbath day to make it different from the other days of the week. We can attend our church meetings, write in our journals, and study the scriptures. This is the day when we are expected to live our best, when we put on our best clothes, read our best books, think our best thoughts, and associate with the people who mean the most in our lives. We should concentrate on Jesus Christ and the sacrifice that he gave to us and remember how much he loves us.

When we obey the commandment to honor the Sabbath, we receive great promises from the Lord. Elder Dallin H. Oaks of the Quorum of the Twelve Apostles has taught, "The Sabbath is a blessing to man as a time of spiritual growth and refreshment. . . . Persons who fail to keep the Sabbath lose an opportunity for spiritual growth and forfeit the rich companionship of the Spirit of the Lord."*

---

*BYU Speeches, September 10, 1974, 218.

•49•
Obeying the Law

Article of Faith 12
"The Twelfth Article of Faith" (CS, 131)

We need rules or laws to help us live together in safety and peace. As members of The Church of Jesus Christ of Latter-day Saints, we believe in honoring and obeying the laws of the countries where we live.

Jesus knew it was important to obey the laws of the land. In the country where he lived, Caesar was the ruler. When the people asked Jesus if they should obey man's law or God's law, he told the people to obey and honor both.

Heavenly Father and Jesus Christ have given us certain laws to live by so we can be happy in this life and prepare to live with them again. The rules and laws in our countries are meant to help us live together in safety and peace with our neighbors. We also have rules in our families to help us live, work, and play together in love and harmony.

President Heber J. Grant taught, "Perhaps there is nothing of greater importance, next to our spiritual growth, than a determination on the part of the Latter-day Saints to observe the laws of our country."*

And President Howard W. Hunter added, "It is a part of our religion to be good drivers, to obey the traffic laws, to support and assist the policeman, not dodge him nor dog him. . . . As people who honor the law, who believe in being honest, who believe in doing to others as we would have others do to us, we are duty bound to keep the law."**

---

*Conference Report, October 1927, 5.

**_Teachings of Howard W. Hunter_ (Salt Lake City: Bookcraft, 1997), 163–64.

•50•
Fasting

Matthew 6:16-18

"Bless Our Fast, We Pray" (Hymns, 138)

To fast means to go without eating and drinking. Jesus set the example himself by fasting. We fast because it is a teaching of Jesus Christ. We also fast to help the poor and needy. We give the money we save by not eating our meals to the fast offering fund. That fund helps others who don't have enough food.

Fasting is a way of developing self-control. If we can learn to have control over what and when we eat, we'll have greater control in other things we do as well. Another very important blessing of fasting is that it helps us to be more humble and to feel closer to Heavenly Father. Fasting can help us to have his guidance and influence in our lives.

Fast Sunday is always held on the first Sunday of the month (except at general conference time). It is a time when we can share our testimonies in sacrament meeting.

Sometimes fasting can be difficult. Because it isn't always easy, we can pray and ask our Heavenly Father for strength. The more we fast, the easier it can become. We can learn more about our Heavenly Father and Jesus Christ by fasting on fast Sunday.

Elder L. Tom Perry of the Quorum of the Twelve taught, "Fasting is . . . one of the finest ways of developing our own discipline and self-control. . . . Fasting helps to teach us self-mastery. It helps us to gain the discipline we need to have control over ourselves. . . .

"Fasting and prayer bring forth a special spiritual power. This same blessing is available to each of us if we will only take advantage of it."*

---

*"The Law of the Fast," *Ensign,* May 1986, 31–33.

•51•
Service

Mosiah 2:17

"When We're Helping" (CS, 198)

King Mosiah told his people that "when ye are in the service of your fellow beings ye are only in the service of your God" (Mosiah 2:17). God has commanded us to love and help one another. When we do, we are helping him in his work.

Giving service is like giving a gift to someone else. It is not a gift of money, but instead is a gift of your time and your love. Service is one of the best gifts you can give. When you are serving others, you are giving something that only you can give. You are giving of yourself.

Jesus gave of himself by serving others. He helped the blind to see, the sick to be healthy, the sad to feel happy. Our goal in life should be to become like Jesus Christ, and service is one of the keys.

To give a gift of service, you could serve your neighbors by helping them mow their lawn or taking them dinner when they are sick. You could serve your family by helping with chores or offering to help without being asked. You could serve at church by helping clean the chapel after church.

There are many ways to serve, and there are many of God's children who are in need of service. You can show your love for a friend, neighbor, or someone in your family by serving them. You will see the happiness that your service brings. Service is best if done in secret. We do not need public praise, just the quiet assurance of knowing that serving helps others and brings us closer to Christ.

When you bless and help others, you bless yourself as well. You'll feel happier in life when you make service a regular part of your life.

•52•
Patriarchal Blessings

Doctrine and Covenants 124:91–94
"I Will Follow God's Plan" (CS, 164)

A patriarchal blessing is personal revelation available to each of us. Patriarchal blessings help us learn the truth about ourselves. It is our responsibility to prayerfully read our blessing to receive the direction we need to fulfill our life's mission and to avoid the pitfalls that will take us off course. A patriarchal blessing is our opportunity to learn firsthand about Heavenly Father's confidence in us. The blessing reveals his plan for us.

A blessing is given by an ordained patriarch and is inspired of God. It is a guideline similar to a road map, which helps us find the paths that should be traveled and destinations that may be reached if we stay on those paths.

We should always live worthy so that when we are ready we may obtain this blessing. Patriarchal blessings are not given until the recipient is old enough to truly understand the things the patriarch is inspired to say. Once we have our blessing, we should seek to live in such a way that we will always be worthy of the blessings promised to us.

President James E. Faust of the First Presidency has taught: "The patriarch has no blessing of his own to give; the blessing is the Lord's to give. God knows our spirits; he knows our strengths and weaknesses. He knows our capabilities and our potential. Our patriarchal blessings indicate what the Lord expects of us and what our potential can be. Our blessings can encourage us when we are discouraged, strengthen us when we are fearful, comfort us when we sorrow, give us courage when we are filled with anxiety, lift us up when we are weak in spirit."*

---

*"Patriarchal Blessings," *1980 Devotional Speeches of the Year* (Provo, Utah: BYU Press, 1981), 54.

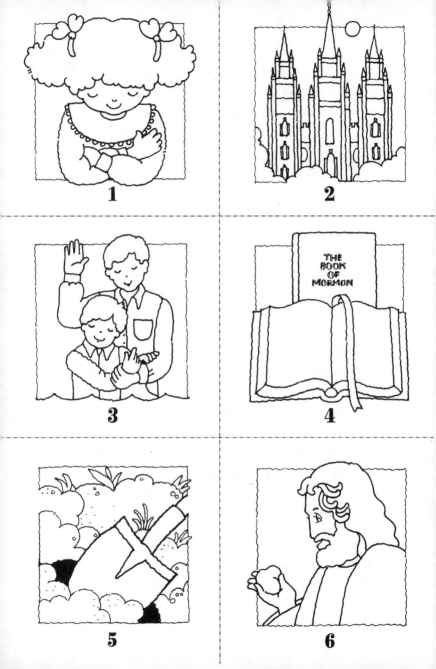

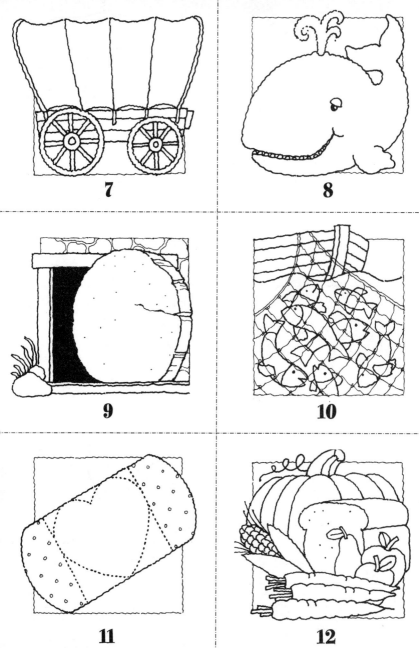

7

8

9

10

11

12

13

14

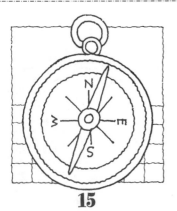

15

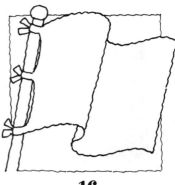

16

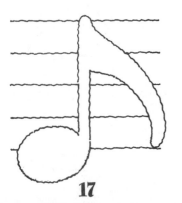

17

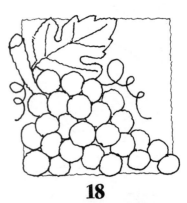

18

19

20

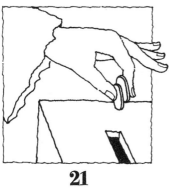

21

22

23

24

25

26

27

28

29

30

31

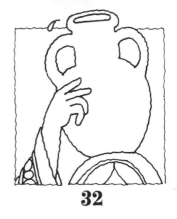

32

33

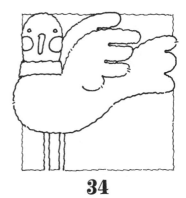

34

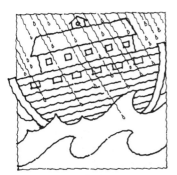

35

36

37

38

39

40

41

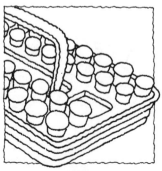

42

43

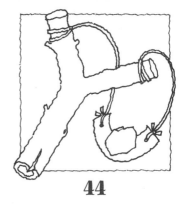

44

45

46

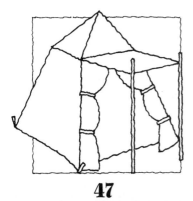

47

48

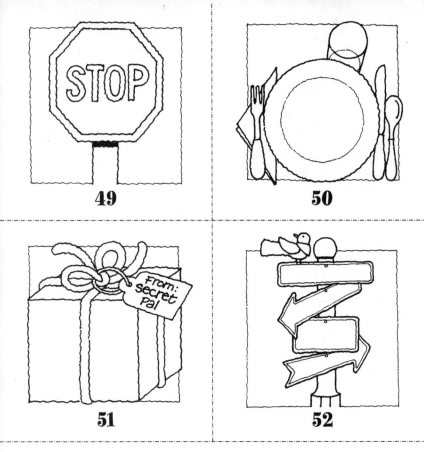

49

50

51

From:
secret
pal

52